# ANKYLOSAURUS

by Janet Riehecky
illustrated by Diana Magnuson

THE
CHILD'S
WORLD

MANKATO, MN

*Grateful appreciation is expressed to
Bret S. Beall, Research Consultant,
Field Museum of Natural History, Chicago,
Illinois, who reviewed this book to
insure its accuracy.*

**Library of Congress Cataloging in Publication Data**

Riehecky, Janet, 1953-
 Ankylosaurus / by Janet Riehecky ; illustrated by Diana Magnuson.
  p. cm.
 Summary: Describes both hypothesized and factual information about
the dinosaur Ankylosaurus, including its physical appearance and
lifestyle.
 ISBN 0-89565-621-3 (library binding)
 1. Ankylosaurus—Juvenile literature.  [1. Ankylosaurus.
2. Dinosaurs.]  I. Magnuson, Diana, ill.  II. Child's World (Firm)
III. Title.  IV. Series: Riehecky, Janet, 1953-    Dinosaur books.
QE862.O65R524   1990
567.9'7—dc20                                    90-2513
                                                  CIP
                                                  AC

# ANKYLOSAURUS

Most of the dinosaurs that lived millions of years ago were peaceful plant eaters. And not much happened in the lives of plant-eating dinosaurs.

They spent most of their days eating plants. Probably the most exciting thing they ever did was to take a swim in a cold lake.

But, every now and then, into this peaceful life came meat eaters!

Meat eaters came in all shapes and sizes.
There were little meat eaters with sharp
claws and teeth . . .

and bigger meat eaters with longer claws
and longer teeth!

There were meat eaters that hunted in packs . . .

and meat eaters that didn't need any help. But they all had the same idea on their minds—LUNCH!

If a plant eater didn't want to become the main course, it had to be able to defend itself. Some plant eaters were very good at this. They had sharp claws or horns of their own. But one type of dinosaur didn't need to fight back. All it had to do was stand there. It was the Ankylosaurus (an-KEEL-uh-sawr-us). The Ankylosaurus had thick, bony armor over almost all of its body—even its eyelids!

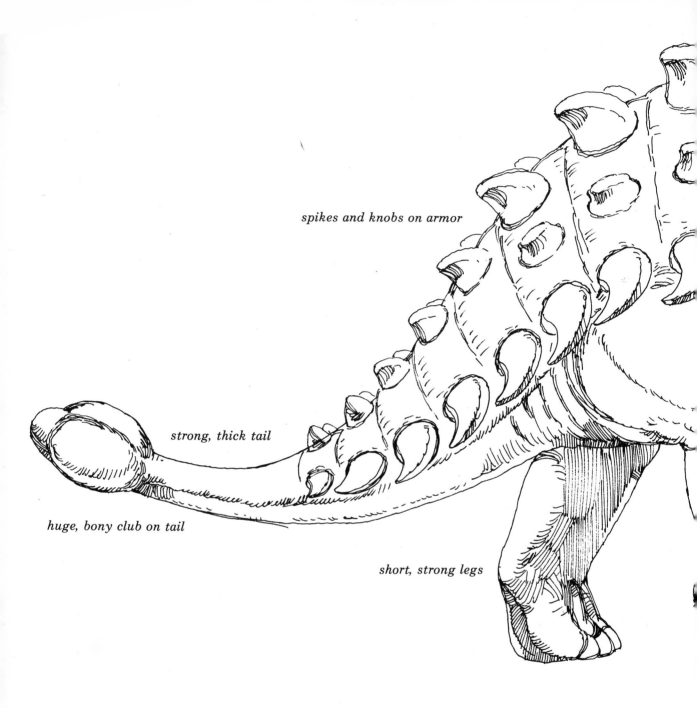

spikes and knobs on armor

strong, thick tail

huge, bony club on tail

short, strong legs

The Ankylosaurus was a huge dinosaur. That alone would have been enough to discourage most meat eaters. It was about the size of a bus—thirty-three feet long

bony armor covering head, neck, and back

small, weak jaws and teeth

four toes on feet

and twelve feet tall. It could weigh as much as five tons. But it didn't look like a bus—it looked like a tank!

Tanks are covered with metal armor. The Ankylosaurus' armor was made from thick bands, or plates, of bone, many with large spikes and knobs sticking out of them. The spikes and knobs were scattered across the back and over the head. The Ankylosaurus' armor completely covered its back, neck, and head.

The armor was probably very frustrating to a hungry meat eater. Even if a meat eater could dodge past the knobs and spikes, all it would get was a mouthful of bony armor—and maybe a few broken teeth.

A meat eater had only one chance. The belly of the Ankylosaurus didn't have any armor. If the meat eater could get to that soft spot, it could still have an Ankylosaurus snack. But the Ankylosaurus could make that very hard to do. It could crouch down to the ground, folding its legs underneath. That way, the only parts a meat eater could get to were covered with armor.

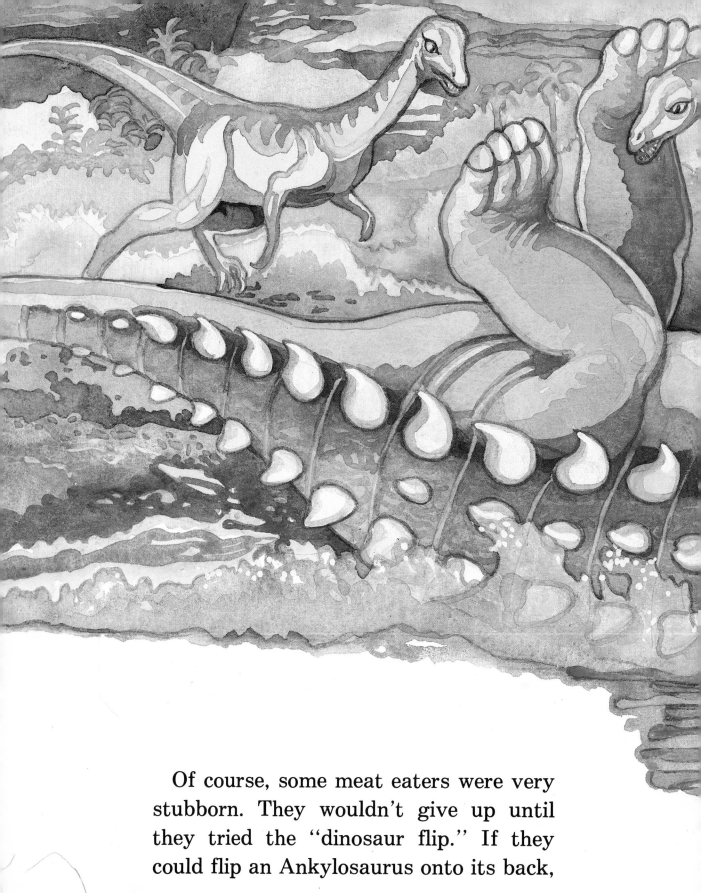

Of course, some meat eaters were very stubborn. They wouldn't give up until they tried the "dinosaur flip." If they could flip an Ankylosaurus onto its back,

it was stuck. The weight of its armor prevented it from flipping back over. On its back, the Ankylosaurus was completely helpless and could be easily killed.

However, trying to flip an Ankylosaur-us was like trying to flip a tank. It was not easy to do. Most Ankylosaurs were much too heavy for even the strongest meat eater to budge. Even a little Ankylosaurus

would have been hard to move. And, of
course, it was hard for a meat eater to find
a place to grab onto it, with all those
spikes and knobs in the way.

If a meat eater kept on bothering an Ankylosaurus, it ran the risk of provoking the Ankylosaurus into an attack. At the end of its tail, the Ankylosaurus had a huge, bony club. The club was about sixteen inches wide and made of solid bone. The muscles in the tail were very strong. If an Ankylosaurus swung its club hard enough, it could probably have knocked down any other dinosaur, even a Tyrannosaurus. It might have been able to break a meat eater's leg—or even its skull—with that club. It certainly could have made a meat eater very sorry it ever wanted an Ankylosaurus for dinner!

But the Ankylosaurus had more to worry about than just meat eaters on the prowl. For one thing, it had some trouble eating. Its jaws and teeth were weak and small, so the food it ate had to be soft. Also, it was hard for it to move its head and neck, because of all that armor. And it certainly couldn't rear up on its back legs

You might think that the Ankylosaurus, with its heavy armor, was a slow-moving dinosaur, but it was more like a rhinoceros than a turtle. A rhinoceros is very large

and heavy, but it can run as fast as thirty miles an hour. The powerful leg muscles of the Ankylosaurus helped it to move quickly, too, if it needed to.

Ankylosaurus was the biggest armored
dinosaur, but it was not the only one. It
had many relatives. Some had more
spikes. Some had few or none at all.

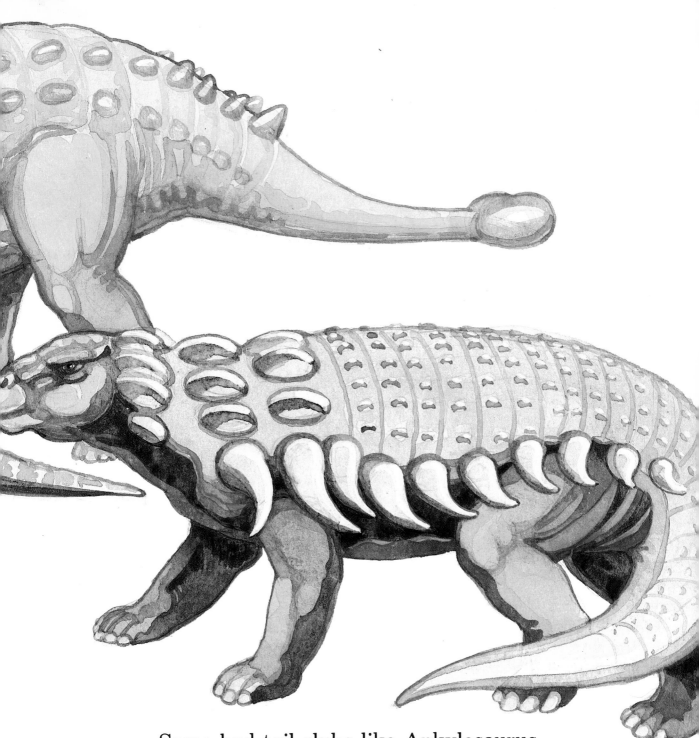

Some had tail clubs like Ankylosaurus, and some did not. But all of them were good at surviving. The Ankylosaurus and its relatives lived until the very end of the age of dinosaurs.

It wasn't easy living in the same world with Tyrannosaurus, but it could be done —by a walking tank!

 ## Dinosaur Fun

Sometimes scientists discover imprints left in stone by prehistoric plants or animals. By filling the imprints with plaster, scientists can make casts to see what the plant or animal looked like. You can find out for yourself how this works. You will need:

— plaster of Paris
  (and a can to mix it in)
— water
— modeling clay
— tape

— a strip of heavy paper about 4 inches by 12 inches
— seashell

1. Press the clay flat. Make it cover a big enough area to put the shell on.
2. Press the shell firmly into the clay so it leaves an imprint. Remove the shell.
3. With the paper, make a ring to encircle the imprint. Tape it closed. Put the ring around the imprint and gently press it into the clay.
4. Mix the plaster of Paris according to the directions on the package. Pour it over the impression.
5. When the plaster is dry and hard, take off the ring. Pull the clay off the plaster to see your cast.